Explore Space, Science and Astronomy - For Regular Folks

Have an Amazing Experience with these 15 Simple, Fun and Thrilling Activities; Safe for the Whole Family

Experience thrilling, space exploration adventures yourself, from the safety of your own back yard or home. Work your way out from there to even more interesting and self-directed activities of your own choosing.

45 ideas for learning about the cosmos - one additional and one advanced activity per chapter - to take this space exploring adventure as far as you would like!

You can explore space from earth:

- Start where you are, indoors or out.
- Search for satellites among the stars above you.
- Fits any budget from none to making money yourself!
- These are the safest thrills you can have with your whole family.

Pick up a copy of this exciting book today and start your own adventures exploring space, science and astronomy!

Your Amazing
Itty Bitty®

Explore Space
Now! Book

*15 Simple Ways to Personally and Directly
Participate in Space Exploration
RIGHT NOW!*

Pam Hoffman

Published by Itty Bitty Publishing
A subsidiary of S & P Productions, Inc.

Printed in the United States of America

Itty Bitty Publishing
311 Main Street, Suite D
El Segundo, CA 90245
(310) 640-8885

ISBN: 978-1-950326-24-2

*This book is dedicated to you! Without people,
nothing happens yet I see group after group
developing technology only, for space exploration.*

*Who will live and work there? Who will love and die
there? For me, it's all about you! Technology will
never be irrationally attached to a teddy bear or yearn
to visit another world just to see what's there.*

*Your car can't write poetry! You can though. You are
a child of the universe. Without you, nothing else can
happen. All the tech in the world is just dead matter
without someone at the helm. And you are a creature
of action.*

It's All About Action!

To find out more about exploring space visit our website at:

www.ittybittypublishing.com

or visit Pamela Hoffman at:

www.EverydaySpacer.com

Table of Contents

Introduction

In this Itty Bitty Book you will find 15 simple ways to get directly involved with space exploration, science and astronomy. Space exploration's not just a rich kid's game or the realm of governments anymore. If you have a ping pong ball, you can play in space too – and not just ping pong!

Action 1
Visit APOD, for Eye Candy

One of the simplest ways to participate in space exploration & astronomy is to visit a website called Astronomy Picture of the Day, better known as APOD.

1. You'll see an amazing picture of some kind, typically provided by NASA, though others contribute as well.
2. Below the image is a brief description of what you would see and some of the facts pertaining to it. The pictures may be historical, scientific or lore.
3. Within the text you may find links to other sites and pictures where you can learn more about the image or related information.
4. This is a great website when you need a quick dose of space, to take a break from your routine or for inspiration. Few things are more breathtaking than images of the cosmos!

This is a Great Activity for Anyone!

- There are some marvelous pictures on APOD (Astronomy Picture of the Day) of all sorts of space views including launches, star-scapes from Earth, HST (Hubble Space Telescope); of eclipses and interesting atmospheric phenomenon.
- Access APOD by doing a search or by visiting http://apod.nasa.gov/apod/astropix.html.
- This activity is family friendly. You get a thrill from the safety of your own home. All you need is access to the internet!
- **Additional activity**: Request the disc! "The APOD pages are collected annually on a CD-ROM, which is distributed free of charge to educators and the general public." ~NASA
- **Advanced activity**: Do you have a picture that would make a good addition to the APOD site? Contact: Pam@everydayspacer.com to learn how!

Action 2
Track Satellites Drifting By Overhead

Did you know that you can look up and see orbiting satellites in the night sky? I mean the ones we launched from Earth! We've been sending objects into space since the Soviet Union launched Sputnik in October of 1957.

1. Look right after sunset or right before sunrise because the Sun reflects off of the satellite while it's dark enough overhead to see it.
2. The object may be bright or dim and it will seem to glide along. Nothing moves quite like a satellite in orbit!
3. Looking helps you find them, a good tool helps even more!
4. If it blinks, it's an airplane.
5. If it's bright and sits still, it's probably a planet.

The International Space Station is a Great Target!

- The best tool to find a satellite in the sky, launched from Earth, is the Heaven's Above website. The ISS (International Space Station) and many others are listed on their site. A quick search will get you there. Feel free to contact Pam@everydayspacer.com if you need any assistance.
- A great way to find the ISS *only* is to subscribe to *Spot the Station*, a NASA app that you can use with your mobile device or computer. The app alerts you to a pass over at the location of your choice. BE AWARE you might only get the brightest passes with the NASA app.
- You can see ISS and other satellites from almost anywhere on Earth!
- REMEMBER – these are *predictions*! You don't always get to see the satellite you're looking for. Even so, it's very fun to look.
- **Additional activity**: Find other ways to use the *Heaven's Above* website. There are many great tools and diagrams there.
- **Advanced activity**: Look into ham radio antennas that are used to hear satellites and if you are really ambitious, build one! Perhaps we could collaborate because this is something I'd like to do too; email address above.

Action 3
Stargazing

Until recently, looking up, and seeing the stars in the night sky, was just part of our daily lives. More wasted, and less secure lighting has consumed our cities yet the stars still shine on and all you need to do, even now, is to look up.

1. On any given (clear) night, you can still see the brightest stars in the night sky.
2. Sometimes you can see planets.
3. More often you can spot the Moon. It's a pretty easy target though – when visible.
4. There is about one meteor shower a month, however the Perseids in August and the Leonids in November are considered the best, you'll probably hear about them most often.
5. On rare occasions a comet graces the night sky. Seeing a comet typically requires a dark viewing site and usually binoculars or a telescope.

All You Do is *Look Up*!

- Your best tool is your vision. Take good care of your eyes; never look directly at the Sun! Even during an eclipse of the sun, use filters made for that, welders #14 or #12 glass or an indirect method like a pinhole projector.
- There are a couple of tools which will help you find stars and other objects in the night sky, see Action 11 for more information about that.
- Binoculars expand the number of objects you can see in the night sky and they are pretty easy to come by.
- **Additional activity**: Tune in to the IDA, a.k.a. the International Dark Sky Association. You'll learn about lighting, security, how to have a night sky *and* a more secure nighttime.
- **Advanced activity**: Every March in many locations in the world, amateur astronomers are out at night in search of the most "M" objects they can find. Find out who Messier was and why this tradition lives on! You may want to participate in one of these events once you do.

Action 4
Enter to Win a Prize!

In 2014, I won a spotting scope and a pair of binoculars from two different contests. I won because I *entered* to win! Often the odds are very good in new or local events, like these were. Few people are in attendance or they don't even know about the contests!

1. Entering contests can be fun. Unless it's especially important or interesting (like the ones I mentioned), I tend to leave this kind of activity to slow times like around the holidays – if I'm not doing much else.
2. While entering contests is fun, winning is even better!
3. Use your best judgment. I rarely enter a contest with a bazillion others going for the prize unless it's really something special.
4. Careful not to get addicted to this. It's a great experience to enter a contest then to win. It could take over if you are not vigilant and you are concerned about that.

Read the Rules and Follow *All* Directions to the Letter!

- To increase your odds of winning, read all the rules and <u>follow</u> <u>them</u> <u>exactly</u>. Getting your entry in on time is especially important! I read one that seemed to go to 'August 13th' only to realize that they *really* meant August 12th at midnight! It makes a difference!
- **Additional activity**: Seek out skill based contests because they sometimes have even fewer entrants and it's easier to get eliminated by not doing everything they specify (let others do that!). Following all rules is especially important in these contests. Don't get eliminated because you '*oopsed*!'
- **Advanced activity**: Offer a prize to others. It's a great way to build excitement for your website or business, get new members on your list and you may learn what is interesting to your market.

Action 5
Do It With Other People

If you are a social type, there are many sites and forums these days where you can learn a great deal by 'listening in' and asking questions. There are scores of people with a lot of experience participating this way and who love to share what they know!

1. First, find a variety of sites to explore.
2. Then, READ THE RULES! If this is an established site, the admin can, and will kick you out if you are not a 'good citizen' on the site.
3. Spend time reading posts by others, get the feel of the forum before you ever type one word and post it there!
4. Start by posting a question, be willing to learn. People love a newbie! You might find a 'mentor' by being open to new things.
5. Participate as naturally as you can. People like 'for real' and they've been getting what they want, if you noticed all the 'reality TV shows' out there.
6. Need sponsors or some other kind of support? Be willing to help first; then ask for help in return. The response could be very enthusiastic!

Sites to Search...

- Facebook has many Pages and Groups already set up to share space related information. Everyday Spacer has a few there too!
- On Twitter you'll find many related 'tweets' at any time. Our hashtag is #espacer. We post events you can attend. If you post events with #espacer, then others can find them too and join the fun!
- There are so many other ways to find these groups, try a search with *alt.name*. Use space or astronomy, etc. for the 'name' part. I bet you have some interesting ideas as well.
- **Additional activity**: Join organizations involved with space exploration like NSS, SFF (National Space Society and Space Frontier Foundation respectively) and The Planetary Society to see if they are getting together anywhere. NSS has chapters, SFF has conferences and The Planetary Society has all kinds of things going on!
- **Advanced activity**: Build your own network or following for support and to promote your own ideas, products or services. Be of service first and your followers will help you in amazing ways!

Action 6
Attend a Star Party – It's the Only Party That You Are *Encouraged* to 'Crash'!

The next step you might take is attending a Star Party! This will really get you involved.

1. A Star Party is a gathering of amateur astronomy folks who bring out their telescopes, binoculars and other toys, er, I mean tools to observe the night sky.
2. Star Parties are a great way to learn a great deal in a single evening.
3. The people who participate in Star Parties tend to be very easy to approach and ask questions.
4. PLEASE be careful around their equipment though! It can sometimes be cherished and/or expensive and while this is a very civilized bunch, you *are* asking them to share their equipment with you, however briefly. Follow their instructions to the best of your ability and all should be well!

A Few Precautions Out in the Field...

- Weather is the number one factor when considering this activity. Consulting a Clear Sky Chart *before you go* can make a big difference!
- You may be heading out to a dark site which can be remote. Take care to prepare for this like you might any trip off-road.
- Consider cell phone reception, or lack thereof.
- DRESS WARMLY and in layers. A hot day in the desert will probably be a cold night standing around in the dark.
- Cover flashlights in red or get a red flashlight. For a recommendation, write: Pam@everydayspacer.com.
- Create a checklist for the kind of trip you're taking then print out a new version each time; add or subtract items as needed.
- **Additional activity**: Target the moon or a planet in the night sky and draw its features or start a journal of your observing sessions describing what you do and see and the equipment you use or both!
- **Advanced activity**: Search for the AAVSO (American Association of Variable Star Observers) and find out how you can contribute to their research right now!

Action 7
Request Stuff from NASA

While there is so much online now, you can still request stuff from NASA.

1. I did that in the recent past when I learned, from their website, that APOD images were collected together in a disk. It's easy!
2. NASA is an incredible resource for learning and developing various aspects of your everyday life. You can receive that information by snail mail, by email or by visiting NASA sites online.

Have You Seen What NASA Can do for You Now?

- While so much is online and requesting physical things from NASA is not as common as it once was, they still offer educators, students and the general public interesting fliers, paper models and so forth. https://www.nasa.gov/audience/foreducators/index.html
- JPL usually has an Open House once a year. At times, they still have posters and other souvenirs of your visit available. Other NASA Centers may do something similar.
- **Addition activity**: Visit a NASA Center or installation near you!
- **Advanced activity**: Access NASA's Technology Transfer centers for your business.

Action 8
Speaking of NASA...

Perhaps you already know about the NASA Centers which you may visit in person. There are a few other things you might want to know about them...

1. There are 11 Visitor Centers and 4 locations where Space Shuttles are now housed. http://www.visitnasa.com/nasa-visitor-centers
2. Over 44.5 million people visit NASA centers every year.
3. At one time, public perception was that NASA got 20% of the annual USA budget. Actually NASA has only ever received about one penny for every tax dollar and they get even less than that now, about ½ a penny per dollar.
4. The return on investment dollars spent through NASA research and exploration is thought to be between less than 1% and over 1,000%. It is very difficult to assess this number. Clearly, the space program has enabled amazing technology. The annual publication "NASA Spinoffs" showcases some of them. It's available online now.

Did You Know That There is a 'Passport' System Tied in to Visiting NASA Centers?

- "Join the Passport to Explore Space program and get ready to explore and experience NASA's universe of diverse Visitor Centers and the museums which house America's four space shuttles! Your mission is to visit all 14 visitor centers and space shuttle locations." Search: *Passport to Explore* for benefits and more information.
- A little planning goes a long way. Website research and calling ahead can help you plan your trip.
- NASA Centers are, currently, in the following states: Alabama, California, Florida, Maryland, Mississippi, Ohio, Texas, Virginia and Intrepid in New York. Which is closest to you?
- **Additional activity**: Work on getting a special tour of a location in the system not normally available to the general public like Plumbrook Station in Ohio. It's possible, just a little more challenging!
- **Advanced activity**: Volunteer at a NASA Visitor Center near *you*! There are some amazing benefits if you do. I did that at NASA Lewis (now Glenn) in Cleveland, OH for three years in the 90s.

Action 9
Send Yourself to Mars!

There are several ways to 'virtually' send yourself off-world and elsewhere in the solar system these days. Here are some examples...

1. Our friends at *Photos to Space* have a program to send your photo on a launch. The launches are typically small or 'Next Generation' vehicles, not the big guys. Things change so write to learn more: Pam@everydayspacer.com.
2. NASA offers 'miles' and a 'boarding pass' on their spacecraft sometimes.
3. There are other groups offering to send your DNA (a hair with a follicle) or your ashes into space and they are getting some serious clients, like Star Trek actors, being launched as part of a memorial service; akin to spreading your ashes at sea.

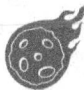

What's Possible in the Future?

- If you ever watched Star Trek you may have seen a body 'committed to space.' The remains of Mr. Spock were even renewed on a planet undergoing terra-forming in one movie. Perhaps we will actually provide services to people that way some day.

- Eventually, many more of us will travel off-world, not just astronauts and cosmonauts, or photos, or our DNA, or ashes. The 'Next Generation' of launch vehicles are being created by some interesting organizations out there. Imagine how and where *they* might send us!

- **Additional activity**: Find Mars in the night sky. It comes around about every two years for a while. That is when you'll hear about launches to the planet Mars because Earth and Mars will soon be the shortest distance between them to make the trip.

- **Advanced activity**: Spend time in a Mars analog. There are several places on Earth where you can go and simulate life the way it might be on Mars. For current locations, reach out to: Pam@everydayspacer.com. Be sure you have something to offer though!

Action 10
Track Launches Worldwide!

There are several ways you can track launches all over the world. Some possibilities are...

1. You can call the Vandenberg Air Force Base Launch Hot Line. You'll only get launches out of VAFB though. This changes periodically so contact Pam@everydayspacer.com or check online for the current phone number.
2. You can read Space News (an industry magazine published about 10 times a year and accessible online in various ways.) They sometimes include a page of launches in their publication.
3. Or you can visit http://spaceflightnow.com/launch-schedule/, the website I call 'home.' The list there is pretty complete though they failed to include the first SpaceX launches for some reason.

And That's Just the Beginning!

- Rockets launch from various places all over the world.
- If you are 'in range,' you can *see* them too.
- In range can be a few miles to a few hundred depending on the circumstances.
- During the day, you must be within a few miles to really see anything.
- At night, you must be in the region.
- Between day and night however, it's a different story altogether! My very first sighting, I was in Arizona and I saw a rocket launch from the coast of California, almost 600 miles away!
- **Additional activity**: Build model rockets yourself, from a kit, and launch them.
- **Advanced activity**: Go somewhere you can see a launch in person, either up close or from a distance. That 'home page' (no.3 above) will help you learn when and where to go. Launches are subject to many factors and can be scrubbed anywhere in their cycle. Plan accordingly. It's amazing!

Action 11
Invest in a Few Basic Tools

While there are many things you can do just by walking out your door, you can broaden your horizons tremendously with a few simple tools.

1. The first tool you will probably get the most out of is a Planisphere. Look for one in **your latitude range.** You might want to replace it every few years because our understanding of the universe is continually growing. Even an old one will have the basic information though.
2. The second tool I recommend is *The Old Farmer's Almanac* by Robert A. Thomas. Get one every year in the late summer or early fall. You may find one at a retail location. Online is another option.
3. After that, you will probably figure out the tools and equipment you need, in the order you need them, because of the things you study.

A little More About the Tools...

- A Planisphere helps you locate stars and constellations in the night sky. These appear to be 'fixed' so this tool will serve you year after year. It's "...a star chart analog computing instrument in the form of two adjustable disks that rotate on a common pivot. It can be adjusted to display the visible stars for any time and date. It is an instrument to assist in learning how to recognize stars and constellations." ~Wikipedia
- *The Old Farmer's Almanac* helps you find ephemera – things that change in the sky –like planets and comets.
- **Additional activity**: Get a hold of a pair of binoculars. They help you find many more objects in the night sky, even better than a telescope sometimes!
- **Advanced activity**: Buy or build a telescope. Yes, *you can* build your own! You can even grind a mirror or lens and build the 'scope around it. There are a number of places that offer Telescope Making classes. Reach me here for more info: Pam@EverydaySpacer.com.

Action 12
Attend a Local Space Event

Where are you in the world? Does your city or region ever host an event where they discuss, primarily, space exploration? You might be surprised.

1. Remember the NSS & SFF from *Action 5*? They both host conferences annually.
2. So does The Planetary Society!
3. Science Fiction conferences are in many places in the world now and they sometimes include science tracks or panels. We used to run one with about ½ Sci Fi and ½ hard sciences.
4. Sometimes the line between them, and the people who are into that (like Star Trek actors who advocate space exploration), is blurred. We see that in our lives too with cell phones that look like communicators and various advances that remind you of a sci fi show you may have seen.
5. It's a great way to learn about advances in science and meet the people making it happen!

How Do You Do That?

- Searches and social media are great places to tap into and find local events or ask me: Pam@EverydaySpacer.com.
- National Space Society has one big event a year.
- Space Frontier Foundation has two or more conferences a year.
- The Planetary Society offers a variety of ways to participate with events big and small. See their website for more information!
- **Additional activity**: Attend events elsewhere as an excuse to see the world! There are eclipses and conferences, etc. in some very interesting places. Where would you like to go? Could you make it a write-off?
- **Advanced activity**: Speak at events and, potentially, get *paid* to see the world!

Action 13
Help *Run* a Local Event

If you like this book, you might like an advanced version too so, here's an example of something a little more advanced overall so you get a taste of the *second book* in the Everyday Spacer series of Itty Bitty Books®!

1. This is a great way to really get to know so many interesting people in the larger community, sometimes famous people too! While it's 'advanced,' it's still pretty easy to do this because most organizations need more help running things at the event and volunteers are *very* welcome. It just takes more of your time.

2. If you volunteer a few hours, perhaps a day, you can generally leverage your attendance at the rest of the event, at no extra cost. It's a win for everyone.

3. There are a variety of conferences and other events you might avail yourself of too!

Some of the Events You Might Find Out there…

- There are science fiction, science and space related events in casual and professional versions typically. Some folks have tried to catalog these. It's pretty hard to do because there are so many.
- Start with something that is most interesting to you. Search the topic and your location and use 'event' or 'convention' to find them. Pam@everydayspacer.com can help you too!
- **Additional activity**: Create your own event! They all start somehow and if you are an organizer type of person, this can be very gratifying.
- **Advanced activity**: Make money running your own event. This requires knowing the market and finding a 'gap' in what is being offered already. When you figure all that out, it becomes a matter of marketing – getting known in the community. Some extra training helps as well.

Action 14
Invest in a Project

This is another fairly advanced activity and there are projects on crowd-sourced sites popping up all the time. They tend to be low dollar to enter and it can be fun to watch them reach their goals and exceed them! You'll know that you are part of making something happen when you add your *two cents*… or a little more.

1.   There's something 'new' going on and it's been facilitated by the internet. It's getting things done with the help of a crowd.
2.   We used to call it *Barn Raising*. You know, in frontier times in the USA when neighbors would all pitch in to build a barn for the new family in town?
3.   We aren't 'raising barns' these days, rather raising capital for projects.
4.   Everything from movies to games to beehives to satellites can get funded by the crowd.

This is True Democracy in Action!

- You can 'vote' on the project you support with a few bucks. Just like boycotting a company used to be a popular way to 'vote' against something, you now have a powerful way to vote *for* the project(s) of your choice.
- The Everyday Spacer blog highlights some past projects. What is happening now and in the future?
- **Additional activity**: Help a non-profit like Uwingu. "For every planet name nomination and vote we receive, we will pay our expenses and then devote the remaining funds to The Uwingu Fund which will be used to fund space research, education, and exploration projects." ~Uwingu
- **Advanced activity**: Get rich! Fund your project exactly the way you want to. This model works. See what James Cameron or Sir Richard Branson did to push the frontiers of exploration and space travel. If you do this, you can help so many more people as well. Make it your own and ignore the poverty mindset claiming that 'the rich are unsavory somehow' - baloney. You decide what and who *you* are, not the crowd.

Action 15
Launch a PongSat for Free!

"A PongSat is an experiment that fits inside of a ping pong ball" ~JP Aerospace

When you are done with your ping pong ball, turn it into a PongSat! Would you like a 'maker' version of this book? With over 120 activities on the Everyday Spacer blog, we could do that, if you want it. Here's an idea how that might look.

1. Since March 9th, 2002 my friend John Powell has been launching PongSats. If you register, follow the guidelines and send yours in, he'll launch yours too!
2. JP launches your PongSat for free though his launches are always covered financially by, primarily, the 'Billboards in Space' customers who advertise on the spacecraft and get pictures in a dark 'sky' with the curvature of the Earth below and the info of their choice on a 'billboard.'
3. If you want to help others launch their PongSats, you can get a Billboard in Space for your business. It's cool seeing what looks like this huge sign over the world yet knowing that it's really just a few inches to a side.

Are You a Citizen Scientist?

- Students and NASA scientists alike have flown PongSats. The students are inspired to pursue more education and the NASA scientist get to learn something more quickly about part of their larger experiment; the price is certainly right!

- You don't have to be a student or a scientist to run your own satellite program! You might be a citizen scientist though.

- **Additional activity**: Build a cubesat! There is a standard in small satellites now which is 10cm by 10cm and a kilometer in weight. It's called a cubesat and you can actually put several together for bigger projects. The Planetary Society did that for their solar sail project in the summer of 2015.

- **Advanced activity**: Launch a weather balloon with a payload of your choice. What would you like to learn about changes in pressure, temperature, atmosphere and radiation? That's what you'll get between the ground and the 'near space' position where most weather balloons finally burst because the pressure inside expands the balloon to the breaking point. The pressure outside gets lower and lower the higher the balloon travels.

You've finished. Before you go...

Tweet/share that you finished this book.

Please star rate this book.

Reviews are solid gold to writers. Please take a few minutes to give us some itty bitty feedback on this book.

ABOUT THE AUTHOR

Pam Hoffman *is* an *Everyday Spacer*. Most of the things she wrote about in this book, she has done herself and you can too!

Every day, in dozens of different ways, it's getting easier and easier to participate directly and personally in space exploration, science and astronomy.

It's getting easier on the pocketbook too; this Itty Bitty Book is a great example of that.

If you would like to know more and get involved in these things directly, please visit us at *EverydaySpacer.com* and browse around a bit, or contact Pam@everydayspacer.com. We have something for almost everyone, wherever you are, whatever you have time for and for pretty much any budget.

If you enjoyed this Itty Bitty® Book you
might also like:

- **Your Amazing Itty Bitty®
  Acupuncture Book** – Rose Gong, MD

- **Your Amazing Itty Bitty® Alzheimer's
  Book** – Dung Trinh, MD

- **Your Amazing Itty Bitty® Cancer
  Book** – Jacqueline Kreple

Or many of the other Best Selling Books
available on line.